ANIMAL HABITATS
COLORING BOOK

butterfly

kangaroo

lion

crab

crocodile

flamingo

turkey

owl

cat

rabbit

shark

elephant

dog

giraffe

platypus

bee

turtle

butterfly

zebra

caterpillar

seahorse

ladybug

duck

bird

axolotl

axolotl

starfish

mosquito

fish

tiger

stingray

hedgehog

wildebeest

goose

narwhal

butterfly

dolphin

fox

panda

horse

rabbit

penguin

koala

meerkat

COW

ostrich

rhinoceros

jellyfish

vulture

pig